W9-ABH-995

# On Being Involved

# On Being Involved

The Rhythm of
Involvement and Detachment
in Daily Life.

Adrian van Kaam, C.S.Sp.

DIMENSION BOOKS, INC.

DENVILLE, NEW JERSEY

248
QVaO

## ACKNOWLEDGMENTS

I want to express my gratitude to Father Bert van Croonenburg, C.S.Sp., D.Th. and to Dr. Susan Muto, Ph.D., for their many suggestions without which the content and expression of this book would have been less balanced and precise. My gratitude goes also to Sister M. Anne Angelcyk, S.D.R., for her patient typing of the manuscript.

*Nihil Obstat:*   William J. Winter, S.T.D.
Censor Librorum
October 26, 1970

*Imprimatur:*   Vincent M. Leonard, D.D.
Bishop of Pittsburgh
October 27, 1970

## Books by Adrian van Kaam, C.S.Sp.

A Light to the Gentiles
Religion and Personality
Personality Fulfillment in the Spiritual Life
Existential Foundations of Psychology
The Art of Existential Counseling
The Demon and the Dove (co-author)
Personality Fulfillment in the Religious Life
The Vowed Life
The Emergent Self (co-author)
The Participant Self (co-author)
On Being Involved

# On Being Involved

**I**

# INVOLVEMENT

## INVOLVEMENT

On the way toward living a spiritual life, I become aware of the relevance of really being with whatever I am doing. To be wholeheartedly with people, nature, and my task fosters spiritual growth. Not to be there means that I may grow less or not at all. If I am serenely committed to the task God gives me to do or to the person He allows me to meet, it matters little what engages me. Even the simplest task assumes a new dimension, a deeper significance. Regardless of its simplicity, each event becomes an encounter with reality, with all being, with the Lord Himself.

Some customs among people in the Far East originated in this awareness that one must be fully involved in the task at hand. Girls in Japan spend long and peaceful hours in the arrangement of flowers and in the celebration of tea ceremonials. It may be difficult to understand how such lengthy rituals do not bore these girls. However, when one is totally *with* the things at hand he cannot get bored nor does physical tiredness as readily overtake him. On the contrary, to be *there* means that I gather together all my thoughts, feelings, and memories. I am wholly with what I am doing, creating, perceiving.

At the moment I am no longer simply and wholly *with* and *in* the situation, I become split, tense, and broken up. This is true not only of decisive events, which may fill only a small part of my life, but even more of the innumerable simple, seemingly insignificant actions and meetings that make up most of my days. The secret of growth, the source of peace, the hidden source of spiritual living entails being dedicated to the humble events which bind my days together.

Take daily conversation. It cannot always be about intellectual or spiritual matters. Nor is it always possible to be witty, original, and fascinating. Most talk is a simple communication of common events, everyday experiences: food, the latest weather report, a toothache, trouble with the people at work. What matters is not that our words be witty and sophisticated but that they be genuine. We experience what we are saying, cease speaking if we have nothing to say, and avoid talking in an indifferent or mechanical way. We are all inclined to engage in social noises, to chatter incessantly without really being with our words. We pretend to be interested but are really miles away. This absence is not a question of the topical content of conversation. A talk about religion, philosophy, or poetry can be trivial, a mere string of clichés which I verbalize without experiencing what I am trying to communicate. By contrast, a complaint about bad potatoes can be genuine and alive because I feel annoyed and say so. I am really *in* and *with* my complaint. Sometimes we prefer sophisticated talk about things we do not feel to a true communication of thoughts and feelings which matter to us. Then, too, we can have a lively conversation about higher things. The point is that the gift of involvement is not bound to one or the other kind of conversational content.

## ON BEING INVOLVED

The same can be said about other experiences in life. I may be captivated by a
beautiful symphony, yet how many hours
can I spend in undisturbed delight listening to
music? I must ask myself if I am also able at
times to pay relaxed attention to the sounds
of daily life — wind and rain, the footsteps
of passers-by, the voice of a child, the whir-
ring of electrical instruments in the kitchen.
Similarly, I may be fascinated by a beautiful
painting or view of nature, but such experiences are usually given at rare moments.
The art of involvement entails the ability to
be as attentive to simple appearances like
the shape of a flower, the form of a tree, the
face of a person, the flowing lines of furni-
ture or dress. Perhaps I have unlearned these
simple pleasures. This may be one of the
reasons why young people who begin to
develop a spiritual life find it difficult to
meditate.

A good preparation for the contemplative
attitude is precisely a full involvement in the
things of daily life. Try to concentrate quiet-

ly on a blade of grass, a humming insect, a flower, or a little bird. This attempt becomes an exercise in recollection, a gathering together of my whole self living *here* and *now* in this moment. To be "with it" means to live fully where I am and not to rush ahead to the next thing to be done. Once I learn this art — probably after much trial and error — I may increasingly enjoy moments of serenity and wholeness. Within the limit of my abilities, I am likely also to become more effective and practical. Being ineffective and impractical is at least partially the result of not being with the things I am doing. Then I easily overlook many details. I forget and confuse things. This would be less the case if I were truly with my task and attentive to my surroundings.

The great mystic Teresa of Avila was an efficient administrator of her convents. Undoubtedly, she was endowed with exceptional administrative abilities. However, her religious involvement facilitated the concentrated and dedicated application of these natural powers. Lack of involvement thus not only harms wholeness, serenity, and joyfulness; it also diminishes effectiveness in daily life.

How important it is, to start to educate children as early as possible in the art of quiet involvement with the things at hand! Such an intuitive woman as Maria Montessori saw this clearly. Many of the famous exercises in use in her nursery schools are devised to develop in children the native human ability to be wholly attentive.

Really being with others enables me to listen — more and more a rare art. Most of us fail to take each other's talking and our own answers seriously. The drone of half-hearted exchange makes us sleepy but still does not lead to a sound and restful tiredness. As a result, it is often difficult to fall asleep at night. This may be because real fatigue is the fruit of commitment during the day. True involvement keeps us awake and alive in work and play and grants us the gift of a beneficial tiredness at night.

## INVOLVEMENT

Relaxed attention in daily life can deepen itself and prepare one for religious experience. The religious mode of life is an awareness of the divine source of reality or of the sacred dimension of all that is. Religion and life are not separated. My daily task and its religious meaning, my worldly and religious commitments sustain one another. I can encounter God in the realities of daily life and face all events in Him.

My spiritual life will be somewhat split as long as I do not experience this unity. It will be difficult for me to be religiously committed to leisure or labor. I may be so afraid of losing my isolated experience of the Divine that I refuse to involve myself wholeheartedly in the human sphere. My daily life may become tedious. If I am a teacher, it may be impossible for me to evoke in my pupils some felt appreciation for art, science, or literature. Convinced that interest in the humane will diminish my interest in the Divine, I keep myself at a distance from study or teaching, manual labor or human encoun-

## ON BEING INVOLVED

ters. I erect, as it were, a screen between me as a prayerful person and the goodness, truth, and beauty which I can find in the appearances of daily life. I make an artificial opposition between surrender to God in church or chapel and responsible fulfillment of daily duties. I foster in myself the feeling that becoming involved in art, study, manual labor, and human encounter means leaving God. I fear that fascination with creation means necessarily less fascination with the Creator.

To be sure, this concern has some ground in reality. There is a kind of commitment to the world which may remove me from presence to the Divine. When I exclude the divine dimension of earthly goodness and beauty, I may lose God. However, it would be an extreme reaction to say that, therefore, I should not be involved in the pressures and pleasures of this world. On the contrary, I should be involved in them so deeply that I encounter their deepest ground which is the omnipresent Lord Himself.

# INVOLVEMENT

As a human creature, I can meet God also in the shadow of His creation. I can speak to Him in the people in which He makes Himself present. I can express my love for Him in care for my neighbor: "Then the king will say to those at His right, 'Come, you whom my Father has blessed, take possession of the kingdom which has been destined for you from the creation of the world. For when I was hungry, you gave me food, when I was thirsty you gave me something to drink, when I was a stranger, you invited me to your homes, when I had no clothes, you gave me clothes, when I was sick, you looked after me, when I was in prison, you came to see me.' Then the upright will answer, 'Lord, when did we see you hungry and give you food, or thirsty, and give you something to drink? When did we see you a stranger, and invite you home, or without clothing, and supply you with it? When did we see you sick or in prison, and go to see you?' The king will answer, 'I tell you, in so far as you did it to one of the humblest of

these brothers of mine, you did to me' "
(Matthew, 25:34-40). Commitment to God
which excludes a commitment to the world
will lead to a false religiosity, to a make-
believe spiritual life.

In a make-believe religious commitment,
spirituality may degenerate into an egotistic
search for religious sentiments and fantasies.
A split spiritual life of religious sentiment
and imagination can be maintained only
when I withdraw emotionally from my commitments. I tell myself foolishly that as soon
as I get involved in my study and in the
people for whom I care, then I have to leave
that sweet world of religious dreams and
sentiments in which I want to indulge.

If, with God's grace, I find the courage to
give up this self-centered world of religious
sentiment, I may be able to develop a true
spiritual life. I may find God where He is:
in the needy people around me, in the difficult hours of exhausing study, in my collab-
oration with mankind for the building of a
better world. I find Him in the asceticism of

the laboratory where I dedicate myself, together with my brothers and sisters of the
human race, to the discovery of the concrete scientific aspects of the truth of His
creation.

Present to God, in struggling and suffering
humanity, I may grow to a spiritual life
which replaces the fantasy life that I pre-
viously called "spiritual." The main difference between my own imaginary life and
that of other withdrawn people was that my
fantasies were religious while theirs may
have been aesthetic or sensuous. Basically
we acted in the same way. We rejected the
challenge of God's reality and sought ref-
uge in the shelter of pleasant feelings and
imaginations.

If I reject the world in this sense, the
world will reject me: "You are the salt of
the earth! But if salt loses its strength, how
can it be made salt again? It is good for
nothing but to be thrown away and trodden
underfoot. You are the light of the world! A
city that is built upon a hill cannot be hid-

den. People do not light a lamp and put it under a peck-measure; they put it on its stand and it gives light to everyone in the house. Your light must burn in that way among men so that they will see the good you do, and praise your Father in heaven" (Matthew 5:13-16).

Does this mean that fascination with study, art, science, and daily life makes prayer superfluous? The answer is the opposite. The more I allow myself to be involved in the world, the more I need retreat, recollection, meditation, and contemplation. These moments more than any other help me to be so immersed in the world that I find at its roots the Divine Will which maintains and saves it.

While I should not forsake recollection and meditation, perhaps I should change the spirit in which I meditate and contemplate. What is necessary is not so much an alteration of religious exercises as a change in the attitude I assume when I engage in them. If I want to grow through prayer into true participation in God's world, I have to become aware of my attitudes during moments of recollection.

Do I secretly think that there is an absolute opposition between my hour of prayer and my hours of play and labor in the world? Am I really convinced that prayer fosters deeper involvement in the world and its people? Do I believe that hours of care for humanity can be hours of implicit prayer when nourished by moments of explicit presence to the Sacred? Do I realize that the authenticity of my hour of prayer can also be measured by my dedication in the laboratory, my increased sensitivity in human relationships, my greater fascination with the beauty of art and creation, my better contribution to the building of the world by mankind? As the Gospel says, "By their fruits you shall know them" (Matthew, 7:16).

Any harbored notion of the spiritual life as a sheltered fantasy life out of this world may poison a whole community of Christians. A community like this may withdraw from the suffering and striving of humanity.

## ON BEING INVOLVED

It may degenerate into a self-centered com-
placent in-group that revels in the pious religious imagination of its members. Such a
society can develop along with this fantasy
life a certain pride in their own justice. They
may become overly concerned with insu-
lated perfection, anxiously preoccupied with
devotions and rules while the world around
them goes to pieces. They care for their own
religious righteousness and neglect the genuine needs of their neighbor.

Speaking of religious involvement, it is
well to recall that every mode of "being
with" is highly attentional. This habit of attention is not easily established and maintained; it must be strengthened over the
years so that I can be with something in spite
of numerous distracting influences which
threaten to curb my centeredness.

The development of habits of attention
necessitates relaxed and repeated practice.
Gradually such exercises may lead to a skill-
fulness which facilitates concentration. Religious involvement in daily life is not

obtained without effort. It arises out of numerous previous encounters with the sacred dimension of reality. Even when I have been granted the grace of religious involvement, I should be prepared for the fact that I may lose it temporarily when I find myself in a new position. It takes time to discover the sacred meaning of an unfamiliar situation.

When I involve myself in a new field of study, I may be so overwhelmed by ideas and discoveries that for a while I am not able to see how this field can be lived as another opening to the Sacred. I must patiently accept this unavoidable, temporary lapse in religious participation. I should be especially careful to resist the temptation to kill my interest simply because I am afraid it will disturb my "spiritual life." In fact I like to avoid the difficult challenge to integrate this new reality into my religious involvement.

Once I decide to refuse engagement in the name of preserving religious awareness, I may fall into the trap of withholding the full gift of myself in the next new situation

that comes up. Unwillingness to commit myself to something new in order to save my
religious participation of the past marks the
beginning of a split between my spiritual
life and my involvement in the world.

My so-called religious commitment becomes increasingly out of tune with reality,
more and more imaginary, pietistic, and sen-
timental. My involvement in daily life is half-
hearted, tenuous, and inauthentic. I experience false upsurges of guilt when I become
absorbed in work, study, or leisurely pur-
suits. In the end, I may be involved in nothing, my existence a living death. Instead of
being a center of vitality, my life is like a
tombstone on which appears the epitaph,
"I am holy because I was not really involved
in anything."

It is clear that such a life is a betrayal
of Christ's Incarnation. The Lord wants to
incarnate Himself in the world through
persons involved there as full human be-
ings. He asks for my involvement in every
endeavor so that He can sanctify the

# INVOLVEMENT

world in and through this involvement.

If my refusal to be involved in anything goes to the extreme, I may develop neurotic symptoms. I am in a real crisis. "Crisis" is derived from the Greek word *krino*, which means a parting of the ways, to separate or to divide. At the moment of crisis, I am at the crossroads of my life. I must decide which way to go. The decision which I make orients my life in one direction or the other.

In the beginning I may not be able to discover the way which opens me to the dimension of the sacred. A person fascinated by a new movement in art, science, or social work may find it difficult to integrate his interests of the moment into the life of the spirit. The same is true for a young man who falls in love with the right girl. It will take some time before he is able to experience the religious dimension of his love life, overwhelmed as he is by strong new emotions and experiences. The solution is not to give up love for his girl but to modify his religious awareness in light of this changing circumstance.

29

## ON BEING INVOLVED

Religious involvement is a fully human involvement permeated by an awareness of the hidden, sacred dimension of each new love, encounter, interest, style, task, or time of suffering. Each one of them requires a modification of my religious attention. Directing my spiritual attention to the new enterprise does not diminish but rather heightens my commitment to it. Full religious attention is the orientation of my perception, thought, feeling, and believing toward the sacred meaning of my personal history and place in the world. Each involvement is both gift and challenge. It forces me to a response which modifies my life. If it is false, my life may also be changed, but in a negative way.

When I am ready to meet what life presents, I am emptied of all egocentric preoccupations, waiting to perceive the religious meaning of every joyful or painful event. There is no automatic guarantee that this will happen. The only thing I can do is to make myself ready for the revelation of the specific religious appeal which is hidden in every new circumstance. This readiness is based partly on my conviction that any person, event, or thing can elicit a religious response. Some situations, it is true, elicit this kind of response more readily than others. Still any human encounter, object, task, or study may become an entrance into the Divine if I am open to this Presence. Saint Francis was the troubadour of God's loving Presence in all the magnificent and simple appearances around him. I too must be convinced that my daily surroundings are capable of arousing in me the special attention and feeling which draw forth a religious response.

My daily environment should not be looked upon as the Divine but a possibility of entrance into the Divine. Every new enterprise, reading, or encounter may reveal to me another aspect of God's presence. I should never identify one task, place, or assignment with God Himself or dub this the only road to God. In that case, I might suffer from religious fetichism, which means that I isolate and make absolute one specific person or place and tell myself that this is the only road to God for me. If I do so, I may be in danger of closing myself off from the rest of reality and remaining fixated on one or more parts of my total life situation. In such estrangement from reality, both my daily and spiritual life may become mere fiction.

Religious involvement is determined not only by the unique challenge of my task and environment but also by the originality of my person. Involvement in life must be in tune with my individuality. I cannot literally imitate the prayers, attitudes, and feelings of a holy person, even if the challenges he had to face seem the same as mine. I have to discover my unique way of becoming religiously attuned to the current of life. I cannot find this way by logical reasoning alone. Reasoning must be rooted in life. Living does not exclude logical thinking but it keeps this logic in tune with my daily involvement with self and others. The power of logic should serve the unfolding of life.

Aware for the first time that I am called to find my own path of prayerful involvement may terrify me. Freedom is frequently experienced as a threat, for it entails the burden of personal responsibility and the possibility of failing. Moreover, religious involvement is not something I can achieve by working at it; it comes to those who dispose themselves to receive it. Or rather, it is there already, if only my self-preoccupied ego, cleansed from distracting thoughts and unclouded by anxious sentiments, allows life to appear as it is. When I do not identify myself with any limited aspect of my personality, work, leisure, or relationships with others, then the religious meaning of daily involvement may reveal itself to me.

Full religious awareness in day-to-day life presupposes that I am not day-dreaming, abstract, and superficial. I have to be alive in the place where I am. If I am not in the here and now, if I am dwelling on the past or anxiously anticipating the future, absorbed in egocentric or false ambitions, I cannot hear God's voice speaking silently in daily events. To be fully present, I must let go, that is, I must allow the stream of self-centered thoughts and feelings to evaporate into the nothingness of my non-attention. When I reach this void of self-centered thoughts and feelings, I may be fully at one with what I am.

At that moment of grace, my vision is clear, my perception is acute. I am open for all possible revelations of the life situation and for the revelation of God's Will for me which they contain. It is inordinate preoccupation with status, effectiveness, career, and moral perfection that makes it difficult for me to sense the presence of God. The noise of my self-centeredness dims the soft resonance of His invitation.

I may not be able to live at every moment in the fullness of religious awareness, but through God's grace I may be able to be at peace like this repeatedly in the many pauses of daily life. The radiance of these pauses will permeate the other moments in which my religious involvement may be less full but still real, sustained by the moment of total harmony. If with God's grace and after many years I grow to such a life, I will finally submit to what I really am in and with Him. Then every day cannot but be a good day; every season, a good season.

The condition of finding God in all things lies not in the sharpening of my senses but in a specific awareness which pervades my whole personality. This union with Him is accompanied by a self-forgetful attentiveness, a profound relaxed concentration on the here and now, a merging of myself with my circumstances and the people whom I encounter in such a way that I discover in them God Himself. This is the contemplative mode of presence, for at its core contemplation is disinterested perception which unveils the hidden source of all appearances. I cannot discover the mystery of persons and things without discovering God Himself. In the contemplative mode of life, I surrender myself without selfish preoccupation to what is, without asking how I can practically profit from it.

The contemplative mode should underlie all my involvements for it opens to me reality in its deepest ground; it illuminates the details of daily life and the relationship between these parts and the whole. All modes of involvement thus become more meaningful to the degree that they are nourished by the insight I gain in moments of contemplative openness to reality.

# II
# DETACHMENT

# DETACHMENT

Man has lost the "innocent eye" which sees people and situations simply as they are within the mysterious design of creation. He isolates events from the context of God's Holy Will. He becomes bound to appearances, fascinated by slogans, fanatical about projects and systems. Such attachments obscure his perception; they sever him from the whole of reality and its divine source. It is only when man distances himself that he can attain a comprehensive view of things, at once involved and detached.

Detachment is impossible without disciplining my outward behavior and inner forces. Passion, greed, ambition, needs for self-enhancement and success cloud my vision and involvement. Candid presence to the Divine in daily life is unattainable without detachment. Thus reflection on religious involvement remains incomplete without reflection on detachment and discipline; for these are necessary conditions of true religious presence.

Detachment is a topic not too popular in

our times. Somehow it stirs up aversion and resistance. The average person as well as those committed to live for religious ideals may feel turned off by these words. I want to live in and through the Lord who sacrificed Himself daily to the Father, yet I feel repelled when anyone mentions discipline or detachment. What causes this conflict? Detachment in the deepest sense, after all, implies a relaxed movement toward freedom, openness, spontaneity. I am in favor of these attitudes. Why is it, then, that the words *detachment* and *discipline* affect me so aversely?

I may be inclined to confuse some obsolete forms of detachment with detachment itself. Concrete forms of detachment are dependent on time and place. Certain expressions, while meaningful in the past, may be ill-adapted to the contemporary scene. A worthwhile gesture of humiliation when people wished to express subjection to emperors and kings was kissing the floor, the steps of the throne, or the foot of the monarch. However, anyone who would kiss the foot of the president or the floor of the mayor's office today would not edify by-standers by this sign of detachment from self-esteem; they would quickly conclude that he must be out of his mind. In today's culture, the exercise of floor-kissing is both odd and meaningless.

Unfortunately, some writers give the impression that past forms of detachment are identifiable with detachment itself. Detachment becomes associated with a host of conventions which no longer have any significance. The conclusion for some is to throw out all detachment. Sheer mention of the word nauseates them. If this happens to be the case with me, I may be able to overcome such repugnance by deepening my understanding of the distinction between the *essence* of detachment and its *accidental* expressions which change from age to age.

I can detach myself and grow in relaxed self-discipline in ways that are in tune with my involvement in the present-day world.

## ON BEING INVOLVED

The Risen Lord wants to live in and through me *in this time*. He reaches the fullness of His Incarnation by incarnating Himself in the various periods of human history. Called to bring His teachings to my fellow Christians and others, I should strive to prevent confusion between the essence of detachment and its accidental forms. Otherwise I may contribute unwittingly to the crisis many face today.

Another cause of aversion to detachment may be found in traumatic experiences of my youth. Somebody may have perverted the true meaning of the words discipline or detachment in order to push me around. He made an unreasonable demand on me and justified his request by telling me that I should detach myself. Parents may mistreat a child because they are not generous enough to bear with his limitations. They angrily shout at him that he needs discipline. An insecure or slightly sadistic teacher may impose unreasonable burdens on children, again in the name of discipline. An unbalanced clergyman may denounce legitimate pleasures to his parishioners and praise this as sanctifying detachment. Employers may refuse a decent salary to employees and complacently conclude that this discipline is good for them.

Perhaps all of us are only too ready to use the weapons of discipline and detachment when we want the other to do something for us. No wonder that such experiences leave a bitter taste. We relive them as soon as somebody, in the name of Christianity, starts to preach about discipline and detachment. Few words have been abused so continuously and persistently in justification of the abuse of man by man than these we are discussing. This is why such words may have a bad connotation for contemporary man who is well aware of such abuses.

One way to overcome the disrepute into which these words have fallen is to be careful not to use them to gain something for myself. When teaching fidgety, talkative children, I should not angrily rebuke them about the lack of a spirit of sacrifice in their lives. Otherwise I may foster the beginnings of that repugnance which people suffer today. This is not to say that children should be allowed to move and talk in class as they wish. The point is that I should not silence them in the name of mortification when my eyes and voice are filled with anger.

Another explanation for the negative feelings aroused by these words may be their abuse in service of "collective religious pride." Recently we have become more clearly aware of the way in which the Church should be present to the world. In the past, under the impact of strife between Christian denominations and secular associations, some of us experienced the Church as an organization fiercely competing to outshine others in holy discipline. They would loudly extol and advertise its value, searching eagerly for its absence in other groups. Detachment and discipline were hailed as proof of excellence. Other groups, by contrast, were loose and undisciplined. Even though the creative achievements of some of our schools were not up to par, pride was assuaged by the fact that strict discipline was observed in crowded classrooms.

As members of the Church, our aim is not to compete with other associations for the most striking image of detachment or to promote ourselves as strong and powerful at the expense of others. Our involvement in humanity should be marked by self-forget-fulness. The Church is the servant of the human race. In charity the Christian fosters all the good works done for and by humanity. In and with Christ, each Christian is delighted when good is done by any human being. In and with Christ, we must strive to sanctify humanity by our loving presence, by our joyful witness for the faith. Instead, collective pride may have contributed to the current crisis of detachment and discipline. For it led to a discipline which was falsely motivated and lacking in the redeeming value of humility and love for God and man.

The unpopularity of detachment can also

be traced to the fact that it was often experienced as merely an external imposition — not at all the free decision of the person who was supposed to "offer it up." External discipline took the place of internal discipline. We began detaching ourselves from all kinds of things before we even knew what detachment meant. To be sure, children are not yet able to discipline themselves, even in those areas where discipline is necessary to safeguard their lives. A child does not understand that it is dangerous to play with daddy's razor. This is only one incident out of numerous others in which discipline and detachment have to be imposed from the outside. Nonetheless, it is easy to see that we may fall into a pattern of external discipline and fail to encourage self-discipline even when the child is ready to assume it.

Accustomed to imposing things on the child from the outside, we may discourage his growth in discipline which comes from the inside. The adolescent growing toward independence may then reject even the idea of discipline and detachment because for him these words are linked to irrational oppression and hampering of his growth. In such a case, a crisis of discipline is almost unavoidable. Sacrifices which make sense in a world of adults are forced upon children and adolescents who cannot understand their meaning. It is not surprising, then, that these words remind them of a host of practices and ideas enforced upon them by well-meaning parents and teachers.

Detachment may be experienced as opposed to a Christian commitment to mankind. For example, one may feel so detached from his interest in art that he cannot really give himself enthusiasticaly to the promotion of new artistic creations which enliven and renew the culture. When this happens, a contradiction emerges between detachment and participation in the struggle of humanity. In such a conflict, the isolated exercise of detachment looks pale and wan in comparison to the enthusiastic building of a new and better world. The victim of this artificial opposition is apt to forget that building a better world implies detachment and forgetfulness of self. Self-discipline inspired by religious motivation helps man not only to build a new world but also to grow in sanctity and Christlike participation in reality.

Another deterrent to detachment is mere austerity. Austerity not tempered by love and humility favors detachment partly for its own sake and partly for the prideful self-enhancement of the person. When I am merely austere, I miss the signs of authentic detachment — charity and humility. I concentrate on detachment as an end in itself, while it is exactly my lack of charity and humility which makes my austerity so repugnant to others.

The crisis of detachment is also provoked when I focus more on the displeasures of sacrifice than on its outcome. When I look at detachment from the viewpoint of hardship, I will most likely experience it as discouraging and depressing. What I must do instead is to focus on the purity, openness, and flexibility of involvement which may be gained in detachment and discipline. Then I may find the courage to bear the temporary hardships which go with them.

If I experience an aversion to detachment, I should thus ask whether this is due to one or the other form of the crisis of detachment. My problem may then be alleviated when I begin to distinguish between the essential meaning of detachment and its accidental deformations and abuses met in my lifetime. With God's grace, I may avoid being caught by the displeasing accidental manifestations of detachment while fully accepting the necessity of detachment itself.

Having considered the ways in which detachment and self-discipline can be motivated, we may now ask ourselves why they are necessary. Growth in effective, wise involvement means growing beyond an impulsive, diffuse life to a life that is more centered, whole, and simple. Running in many different directions, my life is spread out over often unrelated interests and concerns. I soon feel empty and hollow, torn by numerous impulses and passions which push and pull me in opposite directions. This kind of decentered living makes it difficult for me to find a life with God to say nothing of finding a relaxed human life. To become strong and peaceful, I must rid myself of interests that distract and agitate me inordinately. Gently I must stem the flow of superficial thoughts, emotions, and memories that crowd my life. The unity I seek presupposes that I can detach myself at certain moments from the rush of fleeting days and establish zones of silence and recollection. I ready myself to find God and self when I distance myself from the flood of images thrown at me by billboards, journals, magazines, and countless television and radio programs.

If I do not give direction to my life, I will easily be overwhelmed by the sights and sounds inside and outside which ceaselessly assail me. Taking one road of involvement

## DETACHMENT

means necessarily that I cannot take another at the same time. Once I choose to be faithful to a certain commitment, this faithfulness facilitates my quest for unity.

Frequently, I must choose the direction of my life in competition with strong attractions which pull me away from involvement. It may be difficult to maintain fidelity under these conditions. I may not as yet have the inner freedom I need for detachment from impulses. However, fidelity to my commitment necessitates steady growth in freedom from impulse, compulsion, and passion. This kind of freedom which detachment fosters is also a prerequisite for personal and religious living as a whole. In detachment I am not fixated on the plenitude of superficial appearances in my life as if they were of ultimate concern. Rather I penetrate into the deepest meaning of the people and things I encounter. Detachment calls forth a relaxed and flexible attitude of self-discipline, in which all impulses, compulsions, and passions become the "disciples" of my call of life.

## ON BEING INVOLVED

Self-discipline keeps me in readiness for acts of immediate detachment when my chosen involvement demands it. Discipline and detachment facilitate faithfulness to life. They also sharpen my perception of reality. If I am not detached and disciplined, my perception is bound to be influenced by the manifold needs and drives which cloud the true meaning of experience.

As long as I am not integrated, certain modes of living remain split off from the core of my personality where I am most myself. This division subtracts from the effectiveness of my involvement. Each isolated part of my personality tends to draw to itself an energy which was meant to be spent in service of all my responsibilities. This is difficult to correct without self-discipline. A mode of life unintegrated in the person entails an abiding pull toward its object and a diminishment of pull toward anything else. When a person is afflicted by alcoholism, he experiences that he is pulled away from more central concerns, such as business and family life. Alcoholism absorbs his energy. This is an extreme example of what may happen when one is dominated by any interest not integrated into his personality.

A split-off quasi-autonomous mode of life is like second nature. Any appropriate stimulus evokes immediately an habitual way of desiring, feeling, thinking, and acting. This stimulus does not pass through the disciplining center of my personality where I freely choose to devote myself to the central involvements of my life. My response is de-centered. I do not respond; I react. Enslaved by habit, I lose my freedom. To regain liberty, I must create repeatedly a pause between the stimulus which arouses my impulse and my response to that stimulus. To have this freedom available, I must train myself in the art of delaying my impulsive reactions. I can do so by choosing a more difficult or less immediate course of action rather than reacting blindly and impulsively. Delaying my reactions is possible in a multitude of simple situations: waiting for a few minutes before

opening a letter I am eager to read, postpon-
ing lighting my cigarette, keeping silent before answering a question. I may learn to
delay so well that if I am unexpectedly
tempted to be unfaithful to my life call, I
can halt my wrong impulse and overcome it.

If a split-off mode of life becomes quasi-
autonomous, it goes its way just as if it
existed on its own, outside my personal freedom. Such a mode of life consists of a chain
of reactions which follow one another automatically as soon as the first link is activated.

Let's say I tend to resent any person more
gifted intellectually than I. This reaction has
many links which together constitute a chain
of envious reactions. When I hear a person
praised highly for his intellectual development, I feel a pang of envy: why am I not
lauded in this way? Automatically, I begin
to look for flaws in the praised person, anything to diminish the image of his excellence. As soon as I get hold of such flaws I
am obsessed by the drive to communicate
them to the person who commended him so

excitedly. Only much later, when the harm has been done, may I realize in shame what I was doing. The process of envy reaction developed in a mechanical fashion outside the consent of my free and responsible self. In addition, this process led to an upheaval of negative emotions in me. I felt angry, hostile, not appreciated, humiliated, bitter, and resentful. My whole life was taken in by this agitation. It took all my emotional energy to seek for the weapons with which I could destroy the favorable image of the envied person. Ultimately, this negative involvement leaves its dark traces on my life. It makes me more apt to repeat the same automatic series of reactions at the moment other competitors of mine are praised in my presence.

It is easy to see how one complex mode of reaction can become quasi-autonomous and absorb temporarily. my energy, emotionality, imagination, thought, and attention. If I want to break the iron chain of like mechanisms in my life, I must first of all become aware of their appearances. This awareness implies an attitude of relaxed vigilance, enabling me increasingly to spot the crucial moment when such a chain reaction sets in. Vigilance is the first act of self-discipline. The next act is gradually to interrupt this mechanism when I become aware of its onset. The reaction chain has been formed by many repetitions. Therefore, it has to be broken by patient and repeated interruption. Numerous repetitions will be necessary before I can overcome a reactive mode. Such powerful chains clearly betray an impulsive or compulsive character.

A deliberately cultivated attitude of vigilance, delay, and interruption will help to quell reactions contrary to the free flow of a life centered and relaxed within the involvements it freely chooses to make its own. When I am the victim of many such chain reactions, I must find the courage and seek the grace to diminish their hold on my life.

Discipline is thus the overcoming of a schizoid or split life. The Fathers of the early Church called the split Christian life or disposition "dipsychia," which could be freely translated as "divided mind" or "divided psyche." The Christian personality, however, is meant to grow to a unified life. This means not only that the Christian integrate his various modes of existence, but also that he integrate the whole of his life within the Will of the Father. And yet if I look closely, I may be able to find certain forces in my life which make it difficult for me to live as an integrated Christian.

My perception may be so limited and worldly, so superficial and ego-centered, that I am no longer able to discover the presence of God and His Will in all things. I may only skim the surface of reality. A rift develops between my daily life and my life of prayer. To overcome this rift in my Christian personality, I must discipline my perception. This discipline, made possible by grace, helps me to see again with the eyes of faith.

The gift of faith enables me to discover the deepest meaning of all situations and events. Division in my Christian life is caused by any involvement which contradicts surrendered openness to God. If this contradictory involvement denies God and is conscious and freely willed, it is called "sin." Sinful involvement dims the life of the spirit to which I am called. It is not enough to pay attention to the acts of sin which I freely and consciously commit. I may find only the symptom but not the underlying disease. I may avoid gross sins but fail to overcome the binding force of the sinful attitude which prevents me from being whole and integrated as a Christian. Penance, remorse, penitance and expiation are vital in this sense. They imply that sin is more than an isolated act without roots in the past. They recognize also its seductive attraction for my future. Penance and expiation are prolonged forms of self-discipline and detachment from sinful attitudes which secretly poison my life.

Discipline inspired by grace aids in the recovery of integrity. It not only helps to correct my disintegration due to sin and lack of faith; it also helps me to be more fully involved in humanity in and through my Risen Lord. The Gospel says, ". . . unless a grain of wheat falls on the ground and dies, it remains just one grain. But if it dies, it yields a great harvest. Whoever loves his life loses it, and whoever hates his life in this world will preserve it for eternal life" (John, 12:24-26).

Purification of my presence to God and others aids me in overcoming my egoism. It also implies that I must be detached from the need for approval by others. "Blessed are you when people abuse you, and persecute you, and, falsely say everything bad of you, on my account" (Matthew, 5:11).

Finally, involved concern for others implies the discipline to withstand weariness ". . . through toil and hardship, through many a sleepless night, through hunger and thirst, often without food, and exposed to cold" (2 Corinthians, 11:27). ". . . never free from the danger of being put to death like Jesus, so that in my body the life of Jesus may also be seen" (2 Corinthians, 4:10).

Having seen that it is necessary to exercise self-discipline and detachment, I can now ask myself how I can engage in such practices in healthy and effective ways. I know that my self-centeredness is always ready to pervert even the best acts and intentions. The practice of self-discipline is not exempt from this danger. Vainglory, the search for human esteem, the need to be affirmed by others may permeate all efforts at discipline and detachment. I am enamored of my own strength, self-possession, and generosity.

Proud and willful self-discipline, rather than integrating me in the Risen Lord and in redeemed humanity, takes me away from Christ and from my fellowman. Many signs may warn me that my detachment is spoiled by a concern for self-image. Disciplined behavior obtains an exhibitionistic flavor; it becomes showy. I act like a phony saint, bearing my marks of regularity and discipline like so many medals of honor. Even those who are deceived by my impressive acts of detachment are unable to like me genuinely; they may respect me but something in my behavior prevents them from feeling inspired by me. If detachment is not rooted in charity and humility, it cannot kindle the light of love in others. Mere austerity retains an oppressive, joy-killing quality.

Because detachment and self-discipline find high regard in certain religious circles, I may be tempted to foster them in order to gain esteem. A first consideration in self-discipline is to watch against its deterioration into a trick to enhance my self-image. Once I discover how I have been phony and false, I need not panic provided I turn toward the road of authentic detachment in humility and charity.

Self-discipline and detachment should not be regimented according to an inflexible plan. Neither should I blindly imitate the expressions of detachment witnessed in saints or other people whom I admire. Detachment should be in tune with my unique personality and life call, with my level of development, and, above all, with the grace of the Holy Spirit as it is granted to me within my specific always changing involvement in life. I can only respond to the degree that it is given to me to see. This openness for the light excludes rigid regimentation. If I fix in advance what I should do in the areas of detachment and discipline, I may fail to hear what God, in and through my changing involvement, is asking of me. Fixation on pre-planned forms of detachment may blind me to other forms which are more in tune with the ongoing history of my life.

My personal project of life should thus be flexible and in tune with whatever changes participation presents. Furthermore, I must commit myself to those forms of self-discipline which are necessary in order for me to remain faithful to my life call. In other words, my fidelity should be a creative fidelity, open to the revelation of grace and daily growing more capable of listening to the inspiration of the Holy Spirit as revealed in and through my involvement in life.

# DETACHMENT

To be sure, it may be difficult at times to know what is right for me in my unique circumstances. I may have to grope for the way in trial and error, lost in the darkness without seeing the light. The test of the soundness of detachment resides in its results. If detachment ends in exhaustion, depression, bad humor, aversion from my task, and irritation with others, I may suspect that I am not realistic in my disciplinary endeavors. Sound self-discipline is not a willful bracing of myself but a relaxed response to the flow of life. All efforts to set myself in a stifling mold of pious resolutions and practices are in vain. Such willful planning leads to compulsions which limit my vision so much that I may not see the kind of self-discipline asked of me in the changing involvements of my life. Willful, rigid discipline defeats its goal. Instead of fostering my growth, it actually inhibits my unfolding as a person.

The attitudes of self-discipline and detachment do not consist of being bound to an unchangeable set of personal customs and rules. They manifest far more a readiness in the depth of my person to give my self to the Lord at any time and in any way that He may ask me to actualize this gift. To take this attitude is to accept a risk: I cannot know what readiness to self-discipline may demand of me. However, by this readiness I participate in the readiness of Christ to give Himself wholly to the Father in obedience to all revelations of the Father's Will. This readiness in and with Christ helps me to re-produce His Passion in the setting of my personal participation in the world. Christian discipline is interwoven with Christian love. Without love, without loving surrender to the Will of the Father, discipline is dry and senseless. It leads to stagnation. Discipline without love makes me austere and forbid-ding, proud and self-centered, cold and iso-lated. Loveless detachment is a principle of death and spiritual starvation. Unless love inspires discipline and discipline expresses love, each is incomplete, for love is the cen-ter of my Christian life.

## DETACHMENT

If I look at detachment and discipline as a labor of love, I will experience them far more as a "giving" rather than as a "giving up." My attention is centered on the joy of giving in love instead of concentrating on the pleasures I have to renounce. Careful not to go beyond the grace that is given to me, discipline becomes a gracious acceptance of the demands imposed on me by daily life, detachment a joyful response to the Love that allows me to be. Both presuppose the gift of a beginning religious involvement; both make me ready for a deepening of this involvement in day-to-day endeavors.

# III

# Involvement and Detachment

# INVOLVEMENT AND DETACHMENT

A young man is involved in gambling at various racetracks. He has to detach himself from this passion when he becomes engaged to a girl who asks him to give up gambling for her sake and for the sake of their future marriage. Engaged, he enjoys many hours of quiet conversation, shared entertainment, and delightful excursions with his future wife. They marry, involve themselves in the building of a family and the care of their children. This new involvement implies detachment from the many leisures that were theirs during the time of engagement.

A college graduate who spends long hours in the enjoyment of music wants to be a doctor. He has to give up his involvement in music so that he may devote himself wholly to his studies. By the end of his medical training, he has developed a keen interest in his books and experiments in the laboratory. He feels, however, his real calling is to involve himself as a family doctor in the day-to-day care of the sick. He has to detach himself from his desire for specialized research so that he may assume responsibility for the welfare of his patients.

Life is a rhythm of detachment and involvement. This recurrence is manifested in life as a whole, as we change from one involvement to another, as well as in each single involvement that we must temper by detachment. When a doctor has to take care of a patient, he has to allay his involvement by detachment. Otherwise he may do the patient more harm than good. The same is true for the involvement of a mother with her child, a counselor with his counselee.

No involvement is possible without detachment; no detachment is meaningful without a deepening of involvement. Involvement without detachment may deteriorate into single-mindedness. A man involved in apostolic concern for others may become unbearable when he does not mitigate his zeal for the saving of souls. He needs other balancing interests and a sensitivity for the mood of the persons he wishes to save. Otherwise he may preach even when the situation defeats his purpose. The single-minded preacher buttonholes every guest at a cocktail party not to remind him that his glass is empty, but to insinuate that he should fret about his salvation. The school-teacher single-mindedly involved in keeping discipline may fail to achieve her praise-worthy aim. Her involvement in discipline is not enlightened by a relaxed attention to the actual feelings of the children. At certain moments it may be emotionally difficult for them to conform to her demands.

True involvement calls for a vigilant distance which prevents less pure motives from gaining ascendence. A woman involved in the decoration of her house for Christmas wants to create a festive atmosphere for her husband and children. Other women in the neighborhood want to do the same. Each house front is to be beautified with orna-ments. If she is not vigilant in her involve-ment, less pure motives might creep in and spoil the original purity of her project. It may become more important for her to out-do her neighbors by buying the most expensive Christmas decorations than to please her husband and children.

Detached vigilance also reminds us of our responsibilities in regard to other human and religious values besides those pursued within a specific task or relationship. A pastor may be involved in the building of a church, a new rectory, a school, a house for the nuns. This involvement is to be admired as long as he keeps enough detachment to fulfill other pastoral duties. Thus attachment and detachment alternate and permeate each other on all planes of life.

The engaged young man, the husband and father, the physician, the preacher, the teacher, the decorating wife, the pastor also have to keep open to other demands upon their lives. They have to moderate their involvements in order to remain or become well integrated people who can respond flexibly and realistically to the people for whom they should care within their specific life situation.

## INVOLVEMENT AND DETACHMENT

The same involvement and the same responsible life can be transformed into a spiritual involvement and a spiritual life. This will happen if these men and women try to keep themselves open to the religious values and meaning of their involvements in family life and professional tasks. The rate of growth and unique style of one's spiritual life is intimately related to the successive, mundane engagements which occupy his life.

As incarnated spirit, bound to body and psyche, I can grow gradually in the life of the spirit by elevating mundane to religious involvements. I am called to participate in the world religiously, to permeate daily engagements with religious presence, to recognize that all human tasks and endeavors can be occasions for spiritual growth.

The style and expression of one's spiritual life are not isolated from his involvement in the world. Within the life of a man, there are not two wholly unrelated series of events — one of a religious, the other of a mundane sort. A good husband and father may try to live for God; at the same time he is immersed in family life. To say that his growth in religious involvement is an isolated "inner" event would be to posit the notion of a spirituality alien to one's daily life, angelic and out of this world. The spirituality of man is such that it grows precisely in and through a variety of plain worldly involvements.

A young man becomes involved in science. If he wants to make his commitment a religious one, he needs to detach himself from the tendency to identify science as the ultimate and only value of life. This kind of detachment in no way guarantees that his involvement will be religiously motivated. A man may engage in this type of detachment without necessarily believing in God or religion. He knows that over-preoccupation with science to the exclusion of other human values like love, care of health, friendship, and recreation would hamper the development of a full and rich human life. Humane involvement always implies

INVOLVEMENT AND DETACHMENT

distance and detachment. Engagement without detachment easily degenerates into
obsession.

Religious involvement goes one step further and deepens the detachment proper to
all human involvement. It adds to the immediate detachment of human dedication
another kind of detachment. An atheist involved in science may be detached from
science insofar as he retains his awareness
that the fullness of human life cannot be
reached by scientific exploration alone. His
attitude naturally flows forth from an atheistic version of what a mundane full human
life should be. To him, it is a life of dedication to a series of different worldly involvements, each of which makes him a participant in endeavors contributing to the balanced and enjoyable unfolding of life as a
whole in himself and others. Involvement in
science is for him only one of these values.

The religious person likewise appreciates
the fullness of a rich and balanced human
life. Along with his atheistic friend, he is in-

volved in the realization of this life for himself and others. For him, too, the pursuit of
science may be one of the involvements that
contribute to the betterment of humanity.
There is, however, one cardinal difference.

The good human life, in its mundane di-
mensions alone, is not enough for the spiritual man. In and through human life as a
whole — rich or poor, scientific or primitive,
literate or illiterate, successful or unsuccess-
ful — he wants to become involved in the
mystery of the Divine Will as it permeates
and transcends human life. A detachment of
total transcendence affects his life as a whole
as well as the singular and partial involvements which make up his life. This kind of
detachment may be called transcendent for
three reasons. First, universal detachment
transcends all detachments that make sense
from the viewpoint of this world. Secondly,
radical detachment finds its justification in a
Divine Presence that is not only immanent
but also transcendent to this world. This kind
of detachment is the reverse side of an abid-

ing attachment to the Will of the Father. Finally, this total detachment is called transcendent because man cannot obtain it by his own power; it comes to him as a gift; it transcends his abilities and aspirations.

The natural detachment inherent in human involvement is not sufficient to transform this involvement into a religious engagement. An example of the various levels of detachment between mother and child may clarify what we mean.

A mother is naturally attached to her child. Hers is at first a blind attachment, which can hamper the growth of the child if it is perpetuated. In the animal kingdom, a mother's instinct is regulated internally. She becomes detached from her young by the simple force of nature. When young fledglings are ready to leave the nest, the mother bird encourages their departure. The human mother has no such instinct to guide her in the rhythm of attachment and detachment. She has to elevate her attachment to the child from instinctive clinging to an enlightened human concern. The mother must not only distance herself from the immediate, affective, biosensual meanings of the child's appeals; she must also come to perceive and appreciate the human meaning of his appeals.

Childhood implies among other things a lack of power and experience which invites others to aid the child in the development of personal and social abilities he cannot grow to alone. The child may sob and protest angrily when he has to take his meals with the family at regular times. On the plane of primitive attachment, the mother may give in to his protest. On the level of enlightened involvement, she will insist on his participation in family meals. She develops enough detachment from biosensual affection to allow other considerations to enter into her decision. She realizes that it is necessary for her child's growth as a human and social person to learn to eat at regular hours, to adjust to the customs of the community, and to respect the family atmosphere of mutual compliance at table. Her human involvement in the life of the child is oriented by the deeper demands of life as a whole.

The question which now arises is how can she raise this human involvement to a religious one? The answer is not by neglecting or depreciating the common human meanings of childhood but by detaching herself from them as ultimate and final. At this moment, she sees the Will of the Father both as transcendent and immanent in the human meanings of her child's life. Her religious involvement is what enables her to encourage her child to transcend or pass beyond mere human wisdom — as when Abraham urged his son Isaac to stretch himself out on the altar to be sacrificed to the Lord. So too, the Blessed Virgin silently agreed when her Son told her, after getting lost in the temple, that He had to be about the concerns of his Father. Finally, there is the example of mothers who allow daughters to enter contemplative monasteries contrary to mere human-

istic protests which may scoff at such fool-
ishness.

Religious involvement implies one's ability to listen to the immanent as well as to
the transcendent Will of the Father. The Will
of the Father is immanent in the dynamics of
the child's development into a social and
mature adult. When his mother lives in
faithful presence to the Father's Will, the
behavior of her child at table and the implicit appeal to socialize him becomes for
her an expression of the divine appeal. The
religious mother perceives not only the human meaning of the educational situation;
she sees in such situations the divine meaning insofar as it is given to her to understand
this meaning within the limits of her back-
ground and education. Her response is like
that of the Mother of Jesus: "I am the Lord's
slave. Let it be as you say" (Luke, 1:38); or
like that of the Lord Himself, a simple, "But
not my will but yours be done!" (Luke,
22:43).

The mother's specific religious response,

as evoked in this situation, fosters her personal religious growth in a manner different from responses of other people in other situations. There is a differential and gradual development of each person's spiritual life; it is related to his growth as a person involved in the world. Without this insight one could easily isolate spiritual growth from human involvement. A spiritual life isolated from man's involvement in the world might sound like this: "The life of the spirit is lived in God's presence. Unfortunately, I have to be involved in mundane enterprises. I have to leave God's presence to take care of all kinds of human involvements: making love, changing diapers, writing accounts, composing articles, playing basketball, performing administrative chores. Such 'distractions' diminish my presence to God. But since I have to make the best of them I might as well pay the absolute minimum of attention to these tasks. I need to reserve the rest of my attention for things divine."

Such an enforced and divided attention

between things holy and things mundane may then come to mean for husband and wife that they must think about God's love while making love, or for the basketball player that he must recite sacred psalms while waiting for the ball to come his way. While it is true that at some moments and in some occupations one can be attentive to a sacred text or mystery of faith without harming his wholehearted involvement in the task at hand, this is more the exception than the rule. None of us would be delighted with a pilot who would meditate on the Incarnation while landing our plane. So much for a spirituality isolated from human involvement.

What about true spiritual life? Such a life would *not* reason as follows. "It is God's Will that I be involved in my task and social relationships. I am more and more involved in both of them. Therefore, I live a spiritual life in accordance with God's Will." This is a caricature of the spiritual life.

It is God's Will that I become involved in

my tasks and social encounters *as* manifestations of His will. I must often recollect myself outside work, love, or leisure so that I
may be able to experience His will *in* them.
I have to grow through moments of prayer
and meditation to an experience of the man-
ifestation of God's will in the demands of
family, office, fellow-workers, or my tired
aching body. Then my religious response becomes a differentiated response and makes
me grow to my own unique spiritual life. My
responses will necessarily be different from
those of my neighbor. Both of us are called
to respond in a personal way to different life
situations. The concrete spiritual life of a
seaman will thus be different from that of a
Carmelite sister, that of a leader of industry
from a first grade teacher, that of an artist
from the spiritual life of an internal revenue
man.

Thus my possibility of developing a personal spiritual life depends upon what my
involvements are. To a significant degree,

ON BEING INVOLVED

these involvements determine the way in which I will live spiritually.

One may immediately ask, "What about contemplatives?" The personal spiritual life of the contemplative develops, like all others, in response to a series of specific human involvements: in the singing of the office, the celebration of the liturgy, the different stages of meditation, in spiritual readings, manual labor, and community relationships. One has only to read a book by a contemplative to realize that his spiritual life is formed in and through these involvements. "But," one may object, "is his singing the office not a direct experience of the Divine?" Sometimes it may be. More often it is a tedious chore of using a human voice skillfully to sing words set to man-made music while sustaining a tired body against the wooden back of a not-so-heavenly choir bench and wiping sweat from one's brow in a sweltering summer heat. The good monk reads God's Will in this earthly situation. He responds to the appeals of this Will as best he can by trying to sing well under trying circumstances. In that daily mundane response, his spiritual life grows and obtains a form it will not obtain in people who are called to grow spiritually by other responses.

The point of these examples is that I can only grow to my unique concrete life of the spirit by binding my religious presence to my mundane involvements. Usually my religious involvement will follow the outlines of the human demands made on me by my life situation. These represent the immanent Will of the Father for me. I cannot be faithful without the grace of God. He who wills gives me also the light to see that Will and the power to live in fidelity to its manifestations.

My day-to-day spiritual life should thus be a religious permeation of my mundane involvements in love, labor and leisure by living them as manifestations of God's will. When trying to hear the voice of the Lord in my life situation, I should realize that I myself am part of that situation too. In moments of distance and detachment, I should also listen to my reality.

A high school principal in a European country became deeply involved in the movement of renewal. He became an active member of numerous reform committees, read eagerly the new theologians and engaged hurriedly in attempts to update the mind of faculty and students. Soon he developed bleeding ulcers. His family doctor sent him to a psychiatrist who cautiously asked whether he was perhaps a Catholic and if so whether he was involved in renewal activities. When all the information was collected, he referred him to another psychiatrist who specialized in the cure of what he called "renewal neurosis." He had successfully treated large numbers of clergymen, sisters, and laymen.

In the course of his treatment—completed by spiritual direction elsewhere — it became clear to the principal that his involvement was not sufficiently permeated by detachment. He had neglected to read the Divine

## INVOLVEMENT AND DETACHMENT

Will in the language of his own complaining body, for God may also speak in an ulcer. Each man has to respect his own pace. If he constantly oversteps his pace, except for emergency situations, he violates his reality. He refuses to accept the limits which God has set to his life.

The principal returned to his renewal activities but his involvement was pervaded by more detachment. When his stomach would give a first sign of impending disaster, he would close his theology books, stay away from committee meetings which were not absolutely necessary, and enjoy a good evening with his family. He not only kept his pace and his health; he became far more effective in his participation in renewal. His involvement before had shown traces of obsessiveness and fanaticism. This always happens when the role of detachment in involvement is too weak. Such fanaticism scares people away or evokes ridicule and resistance. When he no longer disregarded the revelation of the Will of God in the limits of his own personality, he was able to detect the whisperings of this voice in the personalities of other people too. The insight thus gained contributed to the wise modification of his involvement by detachment.

Every mundane involvement should be permeated not only by natural but also by transcendent detachment. In this way all involvements can be lived religiously. Such harmony is not easily obtained. Growth in the life of the spirit is marked by a humanly induced tension between the religious and mundane poles of involvement, which in reality sustain and complement one another. The human tendency is to make one's limited worldly concerns absolute and ultimate. Religious involvement acts as a corrective to this tendency by opening man to an infinite horizon.

It is evident, then, that social involvement is to be motivated by religious concern. Things go wrong, however, when avid supporters begin to suggest that a specific social movement represents the exclusive path of religious committment. The same sense of exclusiveness can be attached to love of one's country, the building of a culture or counter culture, the pursuit of political or social justice. All of these perhaps morally right occasions can destroy religious involvement when absolutized. Detachment has to permeate religious dedication in its concrete manifestations to prevent a person from limiting the essential meaning of religious commitment to only one of the many possible manifestations of that commitment.

Having considered the place of detachment within each singular involvement, we may now focus on the change of involvements. To foster change is another function of detachment. The same detachment that permeates and surrounds involvement tells us when a new mode of involvement is called for.

To be sure not all involvements can be changed. At the beginning of adulthood man is urged by the dynamics of human growth to make some lasting commitment. This commitment is related to the fundamental life form a man chooses — celibate single life, marriage, or religious life. However, even within such broad life forms, he has constantly to grow by a variety of involvements that are in tune with his fundamental form of life.

One function of detachment is to keep man open for the wider human and religious meanings that are not immediately given in the situation of involvement itself; another is to enable him to change involvements when desirable. This last function leads to a dynamic rhythm of involvement, detachment, and new involvement, followed by new detachment, and so on. This rhythm recurs again and again in man's journey toward human and spiritual growth.

The alternation of involvements in the mundane sphere should be permeated by religious concern. Here again one's spiritual life develops along the lines of his concrete daily life. When it is clear that my life situation demands a change in human involvement, I should read in this event the immanent Will of God who challenges my will to change. At certain moments of life, I am faced with a crisis which can only be resolved by detaching myself from a former way of prayer, thought, or action.

I may be totally dedicated to a certain way of meditation. I enjoy reasoning about my faith in relation to life. This meditative stance grants me worthwhile insights which help me to improve my life in the light of faith. Lately, the familiar discursive attitude does not sustain me during meditation. This way of presence to God seems to have lost its spark and effectiveness. It leaves me cold. This may be a sign that I am called to detach myself from my former mode of involvement in meditation. I am invited to a totally new way, less discursive, more receptive and contemplative. I experience loss of a familiar path of meditation as painful. Temporarily I may suffer from a feeling of disorientation, boredom, and incertitude. However, I have to bear with these consequences of detachment until a new mode of meditative involvement is granted to me. I have no choice if I am to continue my spiritual quest. I die authentically to my past or I become fixated on a pattern of life which curbs further growth.

Detachment inspires me to die to a former way of life so that I may be reborn to a new kind of involvement. Such a willingness to die, permeated by a desire for spiritual restoration, points to a fundamental structure of the spiritual life. In Christian life, the mystery of the death and resurrection of the Lord, which every Christian should relive in his personal existence, exemplifies this structure.

One way of looking at the necessity of detachment and new involvement, of death and rebirth, is to reflect on my potentiality as a human person. Human potentiality is not something inert; rather it is a dynamic tendency towards self-actualization which permeates my life. The child, for example, experiences an emerging potency to walk. He becomes restless when sitting still or merely creeping across the floor. This confinement annoys him. Whereas sitting up and crawling once meant a great mastery for him — of course not conceptually but instinctively — now he no longer feels content with what he has achieved. He says "No," as it were, to this state of involvement in the world. He negates his satisfaction with what he already is and instinctively anticipates a new kind of involvement. This affective declaration of "not enough" is an essential aspect of the dynamics of any human development. Whenever one seeks a new mode of presence, there must be, to actualize this potential, a moment of detachment.

Because man's presence is finite and situated, its fullness at any moment is also emptiness. Satisfaction is pervaded by discontent. The ease, peace and enjoyment of any particular involvement are tinged with constraint, anxiety, and dissatisfaction. No matter what religious and human values I experience in my involvement, my experience is never such that my "yes" is separated from my "no." This necessary negation is at the root of my possibility for death and detachment. I should keep this partial negation alive whenever I engage myself religiously in the political, scientific, or artistic realm. Any social, technical, or aesthetic project may attract me as a real possibility for religious commitment. No matter how wholly I give myself to this project, however, I am somehow held back. My consent always implies some negativity or potential detachment. For I know that no human project can completely fill my need for full religious commitment. Realization of my potentiality for involvement is never finished, whether I find myself in the world religiously as athlete, philosopher, painter, musician, lover. No mode of engagement can fully satisfy my religious longing. Something similar can be said of whatever I change or produce in the world as a result of my religious or human commitment. No matter how praiseworthy my endeavors, I shall always in the core of my being be somewhat dissatisfied with what is established, determined, and finite in the world. My "yes" can never be a final "yes."

Detachment could be harmful if it were to lead me to deny or depreciate my former self. I might be foolish enough to hate what I was then. This hate is destructive and not really a sign of true detachment. Detachment is not mere negativity but an attitude by which I come to realize the ephemeralness of all things in comparison with the Eternal. It helps me to realize that my past attempts to generosity mean neither total fulfillment nor total emptiness but real expressions of care and concern. They are valuable and good but relative in light of the fact that man can only reach the Divine in a finite way. This attitude of relaxed detachment from past and present engagements grants me a certain peace and leaves me open for new ways of life. At the same time, such healthy detachment prevents self-disparagement and destruction.

My engagement should thus not be regarded as something finished. I am always on the path toward fuller participation. I am always dying to one mode of involvement only to be reborn to an involvement I am not yet. As incarnated spirit, I am a spontaneous movement toward new modes of engagement. I experience myself as unfinished and longing to be. For example, after dying to childlike dependency I may be born to engagement as a responsible mature person. Immediately, this stand in life carries with it new possibilities for detachment. Because of my rebirth to personal responsibility, I find myself involved in a variety of positions formerly closed to me. A crisis may arise. Again I am confronted by a choice. I must be reborn within the limits of my new situation.

This constant recurrence of detachment and involvement, of death and rebirth, is symbolized to me in nature itself. The set-

ting of the sun at evening and its early morn-
ing rising, the colorful death of nature in the
fall and its resurrection in spring — these natural events have a profound emotional significance. They are living symbols of the
death and rebirth I must undergo if I want
to grow humanly and spiritually. From pre-
historic times, man has expressed this fundamental movement of life in ritual and dance
symbolizing the renewal of the earth after
seasons of drought.

Spiritual death and rebirth is thus a vital
process. The rich flow of life within my present way of thought and action becomes stag-
nant. Enthusiasm is gone. It is time to turn
inward. Absence from external involvement
awakens me to self-awareness. Recollection
enables me to see life in new perspectives.
This long-range view which brings all things
into focus is the condition for my transcendence of a former outlook on life. In days
of stillness, meditating on my limits and
possibilities, my energies gather strength for
rebirth. This period of detachment, death,

and recollection is in effect a preparation for new life. I am suspended between two poles: return to the former me and progress toward the new man. Renewal thus involves a sequence of frustration, retirement, new self-orientation, and finally rebirth to a deeper level of human and religious presence.

Life is marked by these sequences of detachment and involvement. They may be sudden or gradual, depending on my temperament and life history. Whether the experience is rapid or slow-moving, it will always entail a critical period in which the ultimate decision to stay where I am or to go forward must be made. Every major life decision implies the trauma of cutting myself loose from familiar feelings and habits in which I was safely embedded. I must risk the unknown. The decision to be reborn is my choice. No one can make it for me. To detach myself means to accept the consequences of my new stand, to risk failure as well as success.

The commitment which resolves the crisis

of detachment should not be seen as stern willfulness; rather this "yes" is a gentle yielding to a new level of human and religious awareness, deeper than anything I have experienced in the past. Thus detachment becomes an occasion for a new act of self-surrender to the Sacred, which may be a vital turning point of my life. Once the crisis of detachment is overcome, restlessness may be transformed into serene certitude. I may now enter a period of regained equanimity and joyful fidelity to my new life style.

The rhythm of detachment and involvement thus evinces three phases: death, decision, rebirth. The death phase or that of detachment may bring with it initially a sense of frustration, anxiety, conflict. The phase of decision then binds death to rebirth, or detachment to new involvement, and marks the transition to a new way of life. The final phase, that of resurrection, is characterized by transcendence, transformation, and reintegration. These three phases are so profoundly intertwined that it is often difficult to perceive them as distinct in the actual time of crisis. Nonetheless, my willingness to renounce past views and feelings when these are obviously blocking my spiritual growth is a condition for my resurrection as a new person.

For the Christian, this grace of rebirth brings with it an added dimension: I live the mystery of the Risen Christ who is with me, here and now, and who communicates to me what each new mode of religious awareness may mean in terms of my involvement in the world. The teaching of the Lord reminds me that no way of life is ever entirely free of the inclination to self-centeredness. The purity of my religious involvement is constantly threatened. Thus I have to die constantly with Christ in order to purify my intentions. In light of His grace, I can rest in the assurance that I am never alone or without hope in my quest for the life of the spirit. I know that I shall inherit the plenitude of His presence to the world and rejoice in its divine source. Then I shall be fully in and

## INVOLVEMENT AND DETACHMENT

with the Divine according to my capacity. I shall participate in the risen existence of my Lord for which I am yearning and for which I prepare myself at every moment.

# THE AUTHOR

Adrian van Kaam is a renowned spiritual writer and a professor of spirituality as an academic discipline. Born in Holland, he joined the Spiritans, attracted by the writings of their founder Francis Libermann. Ordained a priest, he was appointed professor of Thomistic philosophy at the seminary of his congregation. His life-long admiration for St. Thomas and his writings can be traced to these years. His chief interest, however, remained the academic study of spirituality. This interest led to a series of scholarly articles on spiritual initiation in *Verbum*, Holland's leading journal for religious education. His superiors asked him to research in Paris the life and writings of Francis Libermann; this study resulted in *A Light to the Gentiles*.

Returning to Holland, he complemented his scholarly interest in the spiritual life with a study of the psychology of spirituality. His psychological studies were completed at

Case Western Reserve where he received his doctoral degree. His attempts to make psychology relevant to the scholarly study of spirituality led to many publications on the psychology of the life of the spirit. After a period of teaching psychology, he was able in 1963 to dedicate himself once again on a full-time basis to his main interest, scholarly research and teaching in the field of spirituality. That year he founded at Duquesne University the Institute of Man for interdisciplinary research and publication about man as a spiritual person.

Continued study and a tour of the Far East, where he lived in Buddhist monasteries, convinced him that religious living in most cultures depends on well-prepared masters able to initiate novices in the life of the spirit. They in turn will foster spirituality among the population. Their preparation should entail an academic formation in the science of spirituality. The Institute of Man began to sponsor an academic program in Religion and Personality for religious ap-

pointed to a leading position in the formation of novices in their respective communi-
ties. Father van Kaam is presently the director
of the Institute, professor of psychology and
professor of the science of spirituality. He is
editor of the scholarly journal *Humanitas* and
of *Envoy*, both publications of the Institute.